Reviews for other b

Poustinia —

"*Poustinia* is not a book, it is a stream of life. Catherine de Hueck Doherty's words are tried by fire—a vision that has survived forty years—a movement now become a community . . . This book will speak richly to all . . . But perhaps it will touch most deeply the hidden poor and hungry who have no words for the gift that sustains them—*the poustinia of the heart*, His presence."

— Fr. Edward J. Farrell

Sobornost —

"There are not so much ideas presented as 'sparks' that fly from the pages, igniting a response in the heart of one open to the charism of such a spiritual person as the author . . . Catherine Doherty has written an inspirational spiritual work much needed today."

— Fr. George A. Maloney

Strannik —

"Mrs. Doherty's books are always best sellers and with good reason. Her writing is clear, to the point, so that it is hard to miss what she is saying . . . Rich in anecdote and allegory, *Strannik* is the kind of spiritual and readable book that many will want to give as a gift as well as own."

— *The Crux of Prayer*

Molchanie —

". . . *Molchanie*, the eternal sea of God's silence where the chosen few are called to experience Christ's utter loneliness and where they are first shattered, then gathered into new being. A mystical book born of deep suffering and ecstasy, full of prophetic visions about the Church today, this makes powerful—and disturbing—reading."

— *Library Journal*

Uródivoi

Holy Fools

Catherine de Hueck Doherty

MADONNA HOUSE CLASSICS

Copyright © 2001 Madonna House Publications. All rights reserved. No part of this book may be reproduced, stored in a retrieval system or transmitted in any form or by any means, electronic, mechanical, or otherwise, without the written permission of Madonna House Publications.

Cover painting by Patrick Stewart

Design by Rob Huston

Expanded Third Edition

First Printing, Jan. 25, 2001 — Feast of the Conversion of St. Paul

Second edition, Madonna House Publications, 1993
First edition, The Crossroad Publishing Company, 1983

Printed in Canada

MADONNA HOUSE PUBLICATIONS
COMBERMERE • ONTARIO • CANADA • K0J 1L0

www.madonnahouse.org

Canadian Cataloguing in Publications Data

Doherty, Catherine de Hueck, 1896-1985
 Uródivoi : holy fools.

ISBN 0-921440-34-0

 1. Spiritual life—Catholic authors. 2. Folly—Religious aspects—Catholic Church. I. Title.

BX2350.2.D65 1993   248.4'82   C93-090058-8

This book is set in Janson Text, designed by Nicholas Kis of Hungary in about 1690. Its strong design and clear stroke contrast combine to create text that is both elegant and easy to read. Headings are set in Galahad, designed by Alan Blackman as a cross between Optima and the flat-pen writing of Friedrich Neugebauer, the distinguished Austrian calligrapher.

To the Reverend John T. Callahan
Founder of the Priests of Madonna House

Table of Contents

Preface 11

1. A Fool for Christ 17

2. I Cry in the Night 23

3. A View from the Mountain of Faith 37

4. Repent! 47

5. Preach the Good News 57

6. Lord, Have Mercy! 65

7. Wars and Rumors of Wars 69

8. The Cross and the Resurrection 75

Afterword 83

About the Author 89

Preface

From my day of prayer and fasting in *poustinia* (a Russian word meaning "desert," or "place set apart") I bring you an unusual word: *uródivoi**, a Russian word meaning "holy foolishness"—being a fool for Christ. In my heart all day long were the words of St. Francis, "The Lord told me to be a fool and simpleton, the like of which was never seen before."

This is Easter week, and it occurred to me that this idea blends well with the themes of the Easter season. For Christ exhibited a greater holy foolishness than did St. Francis.

Can you imagine anything more foolish than voluntarily dying on a cross? I had been thinking of other possible ways in which God could have saved us, if he had so chosen. But then those ways vanished and I understood something of the depth of sin. One of our priests told us that in Hebrew the word sin meant "to forget." It is because we forget God that Christ came, to make us remember. Our salvation is achieved by him through his strange incarnation, life, humiliation and death.

---

* An alternate English spelling for this Russian word is *iurodivyi* in the singular and *iurodivye* in the plural.

As I contemplated these thoughts, I realized that holy foolishness and wisdom are interchangeable. Nevertheless throughout the day I kept asking myself what, exactly, this foolishness meant, for something eluded me.

Toward evening I began to understand that to be a fool for Christ's sake was first of all to love him passionately, above all else, and to be recognized as one in his service, as one of his companions.

It also means to have immense courage. I have a favorite prayer which seems to fit here: "Lord, give me the heart of a child and the awesome courage to live it out as an adult." It seems to fit, because only a child, that is, an adult person with a childlike heart, can become a fool for Christ's sake.

This means to face ridicule, to be singular in a manner of speaking, to be a non-conformist. Each one of these things are, until one absorbs them slowly and lovingly, like a sword in one's heart; and for a long time they are the essence of our struggle with God. Because Christ was a fool in men's eyes we have to have the courage to be foolish as he was. Non-conformity involves remaining exposed to ridicule, and takes courage.

But, frankly, there is more to being a fool. We must tell the truth, as court jesters of old "foolishly" told kings the sometimes unpleasant truth about themselves. This was dangerous, but because of their humility they could get by with "correcting" the king, so to speak.

We must tell the truth to all we meet. The manner of telling the truth will be varied according to the persons and situations. At times the truth will frighten us, for speaking it will demand a courage that may lead us almost to death. But Christ said, "Go and preach the

Good News to the world." This is the truth we must give to others.

Yes, foolishness for Christ's sake. He wants us, like St. Francis, to be fools the like of which the world has not yet seen. He gives us St. Francis to show us the way, to help us risk exposing ourselves to ridicule. St. Francis took two pieces of wood, branches cut from some tree, and made believe they were a violin and played music on them. We don't have to take any branches, we need only let the strings of our heart play music, the foolish music of one who follows Christ until the end.

We are asked to imitate Jesus Christ. Can you imagine anything more foolish than hanging on a cross? Is anything more foolish than spending years as a carpenter when you are *God*? Is anything more foolish than spending your time talking with ordinary people, when the world is your oyster, for you created it? What God said to St. Francis is, "Be like me."

Anything and everything we do must be approached with the foolishness of God. We must approach everything with prayer and a sort of identification with Christ. We must always ask him, "What would you do in this situation or that, which is facing us today?"

Lord, you always seem to ask more from us. We must be fools about money; we must give away whatever we don't really need. We must be detached from it and rely on you. Here is where foolishness becomes interchangeable with wisdom. Wisdom gives us the key to faith—or perhaps it is the other way around. Perhaps faith is the key to wisdom, and wisdom is the face of foolishness, which is your face, Lord.

Lord, you want us to be foolish like St. Francis or like St. Junipero Serra. In other words, you offer us your wisdom. Give us the grace to accept your wisdom, because we are so afraid of it. Your wisdom is based on the darkness of faith, this stygian darkness of faith. Give us courage to walk in that darkness. Give it now, Lord. Give us the courage to walk into that darkness of faith, and let our foolishness be our light.

It is not easy to make out of foolishness a lantern to light our path and that of our neighbor. But we love you and your voice is heard in our hearts. You are calling us to the impossible, which with you is always possible.

It's necessary that we who are intellectuals have the heart of a child, that each of us experience ourselves as child, trusting and loving. Here, too, is that contradiction which God loves so much. He who is a fool for Christ's sake is being intelligent.

In this life of faith, if you really believe, as I believe, that I am nothing and God is everything, and that he will give me the gift of discernment when I need it and ask him for it, then he's got to deliver, because he's God. And he does. But I have to listen to him, and one second of listening is not enough.

You've got to have faith, and listen, and not interfere, because sometimes he presents answers or courses of action that you wouldn't in your wildest imagination come up with, nor would you want to. In fact, engaging the very gift of reason he has given you, you would never accept them! But you know in your heart that at the same time he is also saying, "I want you to be a fool, the likes of which was never seen before." At times he wants us to be so foolish that, beyond reason, we accept his decision and act on it.

Yes, in my *poustinia* today I dimly understood the call to greater faith, disguised in your words to St.

Francis. Help us to be even greater fools than he, Lord. In your foolishness is the wisdom that alone will overcome the world and keep us in your heart.

In our daily, nitty-gritty life there are a thousand possibilities a day to be fools for Christ. May I suggest that you discuss with other believers the ways in which you can be foolish in Christ's way. Forgiving others, for example. Or overcoming our fear of pain, of being hurt—remembering how Christ has been so terribly hurt for us. In that deep wisdom that to the world looks foolish, we should desire to share Christ's pain, and overcome our fear of rejection.

There are two civilizations: one man's and one God's. We are called to the civilization of God. This involves the folly of the cross, being defenseless, as Christ was before Pilate. We need the ability to be a fool for Christ's sake, before one another.

Sometimes what we are asked to live or to do will seem stark stupidity not only to others, but to ourselves. We feel very foolish, especially when the situation continues day after day. We have to depend entirely on God, who says, "Without me you can do nothing." After awhile if we let go and trust him, an incredible freedom breaks through.

We are asked to expect everything from God, to live in a dimension where miracles are going to take place, on a faith level, so that the absurdity of the Gospel really becomes part of us.

I don't mean that we should go and do stupid things just because they're stupid and think that that makes it all Christian. But we must really have in our hearts the foolishness of the cross, the foolishness of being faithful to God.

We can't be afraid of failing. We must be free to fail. We need purity of heart so that we're really free. Then we have to choose to be open to this holy foolishness that God asked of St. Francis and asks of us.

Everything can be so rational; we have to march to God's tune, and be willing to be out of step with everybody else. This can be a kind of martyrdom, in a sense. We are all called to be out of step with modern secularism, with this pragmatism which is leading us to a situation of despair. Through our very lives we have to stand up and speak and live the truth.

A Fool for Christ

I am in love with God. But being in love with God is not enough. One has to become a fool for his sake. That means really listening to what he says, which few want to do.

I have an impossible dream. Perhaps I could say, with St. Paul, that I want to teach "the things that no eye has seen and no ear has heard, things beyond the mind of man, all that God has prepared for those who love him" (1 Cor. 2:9).

I hesitate to talk of things like that, but in this book I want to be free, even if at times I may seem to be crying alone in a wilderness.

St. Paul says, "The Lord knows wise men's thoughts: he knows how useless they are. . . . God is not convinced by the arguments of the wise" (1 Cor. 3:19–20). I am not wise, of course, with any kind of wisdom that the world would recognize.

But I am one with St. Paul when he says, "It seems to me that God has put us apostles at the end of his parade, with men sentenced to death. . . .We have been put on show in front of the whole universe, angels as well as men. Here we are, fools for the sake of Christ, while you are the learned men in Christ; we have no power, but you are influential; you are celebrities, we are nobodies" (1 Cor. 4:9–10).

I simply want to say that, being in love with God, and therefore with his people, I am a fool for Christ's sake. Yes, a fool.

I count money as nothing—except that I put my hand out so that you might drop in it a penny or two in order that I can give it to someone who needs it. Hands to me are something like trays. You use a tray to offer lemonade or some other drink to somebody. The tray exists to carry things to be given away, as it were. Nothing sticks to these hands. All passes to people who need it most. I do not care about money.

Neither do I care about my character. My character has been dropped into the mire and plucked out again many times. I have often been put against a wall and, like St. Sebastian, filled with arrows of hate. I can tell you that they hurt. Many years of my life have passed that way. When I look back on my past, I marvel that I am alive today. But God's grace is infinite; my mind is clear and my heart is open to him. I *have* to proclaim him!

Like St. John the Baptist, I must go into the terrible deserts of our cities and the deserts that surround them. I must go everywhere—and yet I may only stand still. It is my spirit that roams across the world, calling, calling, calling everyone to love God.

Can anybody realize the torture, the pain, the sorrow of seeing so many who do not love him? If you are really in love with God, if he is your Absolute, then the pain becomes excruciating. And you *must* go, without ever resting, to impart the Good News. For this you have been created. For this you have been baptized and confirmed; for this the Eucharist is your food. For this, when you fall, you ask forgiveness through Confession.

I wish I had a voice that could reach to the ends of the world to rouse people: those who are baptized but who have forgotten all about their baptism, those who have neglected to be fed by the Bread and Wine that alone can make them people of faith.

"Awake," I would shout from immense towers; "Awake, Christians! This is the hour! This is the time! The world that we know is crumbling because we are selfish, self–centered. We don't care about the other fellow. The other fellow can go and do what he wants, so long as he doesn't bother us. We are doing our own thing, and our own thing smells of hell!"

Can you understand this tremendous hunger? It is a hunger for God, the kind of hunger that tears you apart. Sometimes, in my vigils at night, I sleep and then wake, sleep and wake. I am running, it seems, from one person to another in New York stadium or maybe on Fifth Avenue. I am stopping people and telling them the Good News. But few listen.

I am so hounded by God that nothing seems to satisfy me, except one–to–one dialogue with another person, in speech or in silence, through which, hand in hand, we go to God. Can you understand that?

This is a strange way of starting a book. But I have to write this way because I am a fool for Christ's sake. I cannot rest. Let everybody see that I am a fool for Christ. Let everybody understand that I am, as the apostle Paul says, not a celebrity but a fool. All I want, all that I exist for, all I desire with my whole self is that God be loved. I cry bitter tears in the night because so many do not listen to him. He is *God!*

What I am asking you, each one individually, each one personally, is this: are you ready to be a fool for Christ? And I mean it: *a fool!* It is not a question of joining revolutionaries somewhere in Timbuktu. No. But it may be a question of renewing your parish. Did it ever occur to you that perhaps the foolishness of Christ is to remain right there in your parish and rebuild it? That, my friend, is foolishness for Christ's sake.

We go and seek elsewhere, in other communities and other places, solace for ourselves. But when you leave your parish because the priest is impossible, is that being a fool for Christ? When husband and wife seek a divorce—is that foolishness for Christ's sake? Or is it foolishness for Christ's sake to stay with the pastor, with the husband, with the wife? Foolishness for Christ's sake is a change of heart, your heart and my heart, from within, not from without.

Don't kid yourself. Nothing from without will change the world. Only what comes out of your heart, your very entrails, so to speak, can change it. The world needs to be changed, now! Today! Immediately! At once! And who but Christians can lead the way? We have the luminous words of Christ that tell us how to change the world.

Remember how in the days of the primitive Church the pagans used to say, "See how those Christians love one another!" Well, this is not said today. Christians do not love one another. Members of families don't love one another. Communities don't love one another. Everywhere there is dissension. Everybody wants to do his own thing.

Foolishness for Christ's sake, my beloved ones, is doing, not what *you* want, but what *he* or *she* wants, and doing it totally, with love. Perhaps the word is "surrender." Yes, perhaps we must surrender totally, completely, in order to really be fools for Christ's sake, no matter what the repercussions of our deeds may be. The blessings of God will come upon us.

Do you understand what that means? He is all powerful, he is all tender; in his hands is the judgment of the nations. Christ is the Son of God the Father, and Mary is his Mother. He is above everything.

Are you afraid? Are you anxious? Are you alone? Is loneliness your companion? Listen. Listen to the footsteps of Christ. You need patience to listen, but if you do, you will hear them. Christ will teach you that which no philosopher or theologian can teach you. Christ himself will take you by the hand and you will know joy that is unending. There will also be pain underlying that joy, because he will ask things of you that you might not wish to give, and they will have to be given. But you will love him.

My whole life is centered on this; I accept the pain and wait for him who is my joy to be with me, always. Yes, I am a fool for Christ, and I am also one of the *humiliati*. In Russia *humiliati* refers to the dispossessed, the forgotten, the unrecognized, the rejected.

Would anybody like to go to an old people's home, where thousands of mothers and fathers are forgotten, unvisited, uncared for? It is not difficult to do that, to be a fool for Christ's sake, to try to penetrate the seemingly impenetrable greed and selfishness of many such places.

Do you have the courage to go into mixed neighborhoods or the neighborhoods of the poor, the neighborhoods that no one enters? Yes, it takes courage to go there. You will see the poverty that perhaps you have only read about in the papers or in a book. It takes courage to enter. It takes courage to knock at the door.

However we must also ask, "Who am I, who are you, that we dare enter the "holy of holies" that Christ loved so much—the poor?" He was always with the poor.

Yes, it takes courage and humility to go there. But a fool for Christ's sake can go anywhere, because people will laugh at him yet they will let him in. That is the joy of being a fool for Christ.

You may say to me that I am neither despised these days nor neglected. On the contrary, here I am writing books—the money for which, thanks be to God, goes to the poor. I may not appear to you to be poor, but please come and see. See my utter poverty and foolishness; see a Russian fool who lives in America, one who is joined by other fools. Come and see. Put your fingers in my wounds. They are deep. I accepted those wounds. I desired them because they were like the wounds of Christ.

I come to him and say, "Lord, I want to proclaim your Good News from the highest towers. Give me a tower, and if you haven't got a tower, give me the corner of a street. Give me a poor home or a rich home. Wherever I go, I shall be a fool for you so that I can proclaim your luminous, tender, beautiful, loving doctrine to the whole world. Help me, O Lord, to really be a fool for your sake!"

I Cry in the Night

It is useless to deny it: I cry in the night. True, we Russians observe many vigils, nights of prayer and watchful wakefullness, before great feasts and at other times. Perhaps my tears are a heritage of my people or perhaps they are a gift of God, I wouldn't know. All I know is that I cry in the night. Wouldn't you, beholding a world about to crash? But what is important is that this world does not love God. Wouldn't you cry in the night if you knew that your Beloved was not loved? Wouldn't you?

There is an agony that cannot be told in writing or in words. It is the agony of soul and heart of a person in love with God, one who stands at the corner of streets and thoroughfares, in big cities and little towns, begging, imploring, cajoling, crying out, "Listen to me! Listen to the words that come through my heart. They are not my words. They are the words of God. He wants to be loved. He came into this world to redeem it, to make us love one another. He died on the cross out of love for us."

But, alas, in the dark night, on the corners of lighted streets in big cities or along the paths of rural areas, few answer. In fact, the majority pass me by and wonder if I shouldn't be sent to a psychiatric hospital!

Maybe I should. Maybe that is the place for me. Honestly and truthfully, I don't care if it is. I want to make God loved by people whom he has redeemed. I want to preach the Good News to the poor—and who among us isn't poor? I want to throw my life at Christ's feet and sing and sing that I give him such a small thing! For what is a life in the face of God's tremendous gift to us?

Oh, my friends, can you understand this agony? Come, share it with me. Let us enter into the pain of Christ. Let us go deeply into it. Yes, let us. Because right now, when the world is about to change so completely, to whom shall we go? Tell me, my friends. St. Peter was asked by Christ if he, too, wanted to leave him, and the reply still echoes in our hearts: "Lord, to whom shall we go? You have the message of eternal life, and we have come to know that you are the Holy One of God." (John 6:68–69)

I really don't know what possesses me to write a book like this. But I am compelled to write it. The nights are so dark, and they are wetted by my tears.

Perhaps my tears make the desert bloom, although I don't perceive it. I cannot see the flowers. I am calling, calling into the wind. I am calling for people to love one another as Christ loves us. I am calling into the wind of the Holy Spirit that he may carry my words some place, somewhere, at some time, for people to enter into the era of peace.

Even as I do this, I hear the marching feet of war. I hear, as I heard for so many years, guns going off, and I know that somebody has died. I hear machine guns, and

I know that many have died. I hear grenades, and I cannot count how many are wounded.

"Awake," I tell the world, "Awake! Don't sleep! This is not the time for sleeping. This is the time for praying. Come, those of you who believe. Come and join me. Let us pray together."

Yes, we are the *humiliati*: the forgotten, the dispossessed, the good-for-nothing, akin to prostitutes and thieves, those who are rejected by society. Have you ever been rejected? Do you know about rejection? Do you understand what it means to be rejected? If you do, come and join me. Come and join the *humiliati*.

The voice of Christ has been carried by the wind of the Spirit, straight to you. You cannot say, as I cannot, that we did not hear the Gospel, that we do not know it. We do. But we do not want to act on it. Because if we do, we shall be rejected by our peers. But did it ever occur to you that he who is rejected becomes one of the humble, the lonely, the forgotten ones? And he who becomes one with them becomes one with Christ. Did you forget that he used to sup with them?

Look. The table was laid. All was ready. But few came. And so the master of the house sent out his servants to look for guests for his banquet from among the people who didn't amount to a row of beans. He told his servants to look under the hedges and in dark corners. He told them to find the outcasts and he made a sumptuous repast for them. (Luke 14:15–21)

I stand at the door and knock, trying to wake up anyone, and bring them to partake in the supper. But everybody is so busy about non-essential things; God is forgotten. *Kyrie elesion!* Lord, have mercy on us!

Listen! Open your eyes, which are heavy with sleep, and listen. Forget the woman in your chambers. She is not even your wife. You just shacked up with her, flaunting your adultery in God's face. Get the sleep out of your eyes and listen. You will hear the most extraordinary thing that you ever heard. You will hear Christ holding cords in his hands and chasing money lenders out of his Father's temple.

Did it ever occur to you that the same thing is happening here and now?

For if you listen, you can hear cords hitting human flesh. And you can see pigeons and other animals, bought for sacrifice at a price, scattered around. Modern man, are you listening? Because if there were ever moneylenders and buyers and sellers around God's temple, it is now. Look! They are selling and buying, all at a profit for themselves.

The Gospel is not preached to the poor anymore. The Gospel preachers have gone over to the wide path that does not lead to God. He said, "It is a narrow path and a hard road that leads to life," (Matt. 7:14) but modern preachers seek the wide road, the easy path, and they too, with a few exceptions, make millions out of the hopes of people. And their hopes are crushed. Look, look around you and see what is happening everywhere. People sell anything and everything; they will even sell their souls to Satan.

There has been war after war in the twentieth century, always a war—to save democracy or whatever. But that is not what God asks, whispers, shouts. God asks for an open heart, for my heart and your heart to be totally his. For this he came; for this he died on the cross. For this he rose from the dead and is always in our midst.

Not many generations ago there were still farms that belonged to families. Now corporations have bought them up and become absentee landlords who make a profit out of every egg a hen lays. Now hens are enclosed, to lay faster, to make more profits for the owner, whereas before, hens were free to peck for food wherever they wanted, and children used to go around to find the eggs they laid.

Take a trip, while there is still gasoline to take a trip. Go around and see the churches. They are half empty, my friends, because we do not understand, or perhaps we do not want to understand, that all things must come through the Church. The Church is the Bride of Christ, the Church is the People of God, the Church is Christ's Mystical Body. All things must come to him through her.

While the Pope blesses the "charismatic renewal," I am sure he expects it to come forth from the womb of the Church. It is not something separate, but part and parcel of a renewal that God is trying to bring to us. It must come through the Church. And as it comes from the womb of the Church it will be blessed, because that is the way all movements that restored the Church through the ages have come. It must be gathered into the Catholic Church, and from thence it must spread, with the Pope's blessing, across the world, as it is already doing.

But alas, even the charismatic renewal, or all the other renewal movements that float around, are not the essence of what God wants. God wants *you*. He wants you to open your heart to him, and what is more, he wants you to open your heart to your neighbor, to your brother, to your sister, for we are all brothers and sisters before God.

Yes, as he looks over the world, he sees so few attending to his will. He sees the majority attending to *their* will. God is forgotten, or seems to be.

Christians, awake, arise! Come out of the chambers of illicit sex. Come out from the marketplace where you trade your corrupt money. Come out! Go inside the Church. Prostrate yourself. Ask God to forgive you. Receive his Bread and Wine. And upon doing so, go forth into the highways and byways of the world and preach the Gospel you have received to all you come across. This is the hour. It might be too late tomorrow.

Today people are vainly seeking a goal for their lives. Counselors, and people who listen because they love, are overwhelmed by the tragedy that fills the lives of those who come to talk to them.

From all over the world, especially from Canada and America, comes the cry, night and day, of loneliness. The more gadgets we invent, the more lonely we become. People enter fearfully the world of babyhood, of childhood, of adolescence, and of adulthood. Fear dominates everywhere and loneliness walks with it. People feel rejected, unloved, from the moment they are born.

One woman came to me and said, "You know, I am the only one who survived." I said, "Oh, have you been in an automobile or an airplane accident?" "Oh no," she said, "My mother aborted all my sisters and brothers, but somehow she didn't abort me, and I survived. So here I am."

This woman survived the slaughter of the innocents. Reread the birth of Christ in the Gospel. Reread how Herod sent out his henchmen to kill the infants who were his contemporaries (Matt. 2). Reread how Jesus and Mary and Joseph became refugees. They were survivors.

They escaped the slaughter because God protected them. I call Our Lady and St. Joseph patrons of refugees. I am a refugee myself; I survived.

The Russian refugees—there were ten to twenty million of us—all seem part of a history that nobody hears of unless they take a history course. Waves upon waves of Jews came to America, those who survived the slaughter of Hitler. After that, like a sea, came "the boat people": refugees from Thailand, Cambodians, Somalians, Cubans. The means of transportation makes no difference to those fleeing disaster.

Today the whole picture of the world is changing. Refugees are everywhere. It won't be long before the Third World will be in charge of what used to be the First World. Yes, we have sucked the Third World dry. We have trampled its face in the mud, as Pope Pius XII put it, and now we are reaping the reward of our selfishness and greed. True, North America accepts some refugees, but we are very careful about whom and why and when.

The face of the whole world will change because the people who were downtrodden have arisen. The people who were completely rejected in South Africa and in Rhodesia will have become the people in charge. And so it will go, because the Lord God Sabaoth does not bear that kind of injustice forever. He intervenes at the most unexpected moments.

Listen again. Listen again, man of today, woman of today, youth of today. Hear the word of the Lord. "Hear the word of the Lord, you rulers of Sodom; listen to the command of our God, you people of Gomorrah. Your hands are covered with blood, wash, make yourselves clean. Take your wrongdoing out of my sight. Cease to do evil. Learn to do good, search for justice, help the oppressed, be just to the orphan, plead for the widow." (Isa. 1:10,16–17)

These are powerful words. This is the time to listen to the prophets, to look at our world and to understand that it has become another Sodom and another Gomorrah.

If you don't know what I am speaking about, read Isaiah, chapter 1, verses 10 to 20, and find out, because the resemblance between the two cities and our magnificent cities of highrises is very great.

To whom shall we turn? What shall we do? First and foremost, let us turn to God in prayer, imploring his forgiveness. For in the same book of the prophet Isaiah, God, in his infinite mercy, says, "Come now, let us talk this over. Though your sins are like scarlet, they shall be as white as snow; though they are red as crimson, they shall be like wool" (Isa. 1:8).

Here is the mercy of God touching the heart of man—if he will listen. It is time to listen to what God says. And it is also the time to choose to live in Gospel poverty, identifying oneself, not necessarily with the poor (although that has to be there too) but with the poor in spirit.

Down, down now, with pride of achievements, with money, marvelous homes, everything that can be destroyed so easily, and has been in the floods of California and other parts of the world. Many of those towns, you might say, are no more. Money can rebuild them. But should they be rebuilt? They are towns in which proud men show off their houses and cars and finely clothed women.

This is the time for sackcloth and ashes. This is the time for giving away, not only one's surplus, but one's necessities. Yes, this is the time of ashes and sackcloth and, above all, tears. Tears of repentance, tears of sorrow for what we have done and not done to our brothers and sisters.

Come. Let us go to the Church. Let us go anyplace and begin to weep. Let us together cry in the night. Yes, let us go to church and weep. For there is so much that we have to weep over! To begin with, we have to weep over ourselves for all the things that we have failed to do for our brothers and sisters. Then we must begin to weep over our neighbors, and our neighbors are many: the Pope, the cardinals, the bishops, the priests, the laity. They are all our neighbors.

Do you understand what I am trying to say? It comes out of my vigils in the darkness of the night, when I cannot sleep, and I behold the bishops and archbishops and cardinals of the Church, realizing that not all of them have the gift of leadership.

I suddenly see them as one, those men of God. In them is vested the fullness of the power of Christ. Do we understand that? Or have we forgotten all that we have been taught? It seems to me as if we have. The Pope, the cardinals, the bishops—somehow they all seem to blend into one person: Jesus Christ. They cease to be what they are. Perhaps they don't even realize this themselves. But because you and I do, we must speak of it. We must speak loudly, profoundly, constantly, because they are our shepherds.

In biblical times, shepherds always walked ahead of their flocks. So too, the leaders of the Church must walk ahead of their flock, in total loneliness, so that we can follow them. And in order to be able to follow them, we must not judge them, either intellectually or theologically or morally. The only judgment we can use is the judgment of mercy and love, and the deep understanding of who they are. Even if *they* don't know exactly who they are, it makes no difference. They *are* Christ and they have his power.

Alas, they don't always use it for Christ's flock. We have to pray that they do because, of all the people in the world, they are the great healers of mankind: healers of the mind, healers of the body, healers of the emotions, healers of the heart, healers of the spirit. Yes, that is what they are. That is what St. Peter was, and what St. Paul was. Peter's shadow fell on someone and that person became whole. All these leaders who represent Christ are masters of inner healing, even if they may not know it.

A bishop is an awesome reality. Fat, thin, old, young, brilliant, not too brilliant—none of this makes any difference. Once this man is elevated to the bishopric by the Pope, then his face, no matter what it looks like, is the face of Christ. He has, in his earthly hands, the powers of Christ. What he binds is bound. What he unbinds is unbound. In his ears echo the words of Christ to St. Peter: "Whatever you bind on earth shall be considered bound in heaven; whatever you loose on earth shall be considered loosed in heaven" (Matt. 16:19).

I paused and thought of the bishops who had been martyred over the centuries, and more recently in Russia, especially; they were humble men, in little-known dioceses.

Suddenly, I began to cry. I was astonished to see that my tears were bloody. I didn't quite understand why, except that I have suffered for the bishops so much. They were very close to me. I prayed for them daily. Perhaps that is why my tears were tinged pink, like the red of their blood, I don't know. It is one of the mysteries of God and it has gone on for a very long time. I can write a litany of all the bishops I have prayed for from the beginning of our Apostolate in 1930; I can tell you all their names.

There is something so deep in that mystery of the bishops and Christ that I cannot approach it. The place is too holy. It is not a question of a fire that might devour you. It is a question of walking in tears and feeling that your limbs are beginning to burn. You cannot take it. You run away. I know I did. I ran out of the sacred circle that is the pain of the bishop; I knelt outside it. I cried to the Lord, "*Kyrie eleison. Christe eleison. Kyrie eleison.*" Then I noticed that I had stopped speaking Greek and was praying in Russian: "*Gospodi pomiluj. Gospodi pomiluj. Gospodi pomiluj.*" Lord have mercy.

Yes, the office of bishop is a great mystery. For the man might be evil. He might be a saint. He might be neither. He might be just an ordinary kind of fellow. But as long as he is on earth, once he has been named bishop, he is Christ on earth.

I turned my face toward the Lord and asked, "Isn't it so, Lord? Am I right or am I wrong?" The answer came to me in the wind: "You are right. I am everywhere and in everyone; but above all I am in my bishops. It is especially through them that I can be compassionate, loving, forgiving. It is especially through them that I can bring forth repentance from the heart of man."

A bishop is like a tree of reconciliation. In his shadow, things change, things begin to assume their true proportion. Christ has given him so many powers. This strange person who is elevated to a very high rank by Christ himself effects reconciliation between God and man.

Sometimes I want to cry out to the bishops and archbishops and cardinals and even to the Pope. Such is my temerity, such is my courage, such is my boldness, that I dare to call out from the top of this immense mountain to make them understand who they are and what they can do. In himself, each of them represents Christ. They are the real healers of mankind, because they are Christs. That is the way it is. My heart cries it out. I have to speak these words because if I don't, I will die.

Priests, who are ordained by bishops, also have powers. All of them, from the Pope to the last priest in the most obscure parish, have the power of Christ.

And every baptized person has the power to love God and neighbor. That is the essence of baptism. We were placed in the baptismal water of Jesus Christ and we rose clean and fresh. As we grow older, we also grow in the power of proclaiming the Word of God.

Doesn't it tear you apart to see that so few proclaim it? Doesn't it break your heart to see that some reject the Word of God, allow it die, just as described in the parable of the sower? (Mt 13:4–23) Doesn't it break your heart to hear atheists deride Christ? However, atheism can be conquered.

But apathy and self–will and the desire to "do one's own thing"—those are very hard to conquer. Because then man pits his will against God's will. What can one do with that? What is one to do, when the words of

Christ do not bear fruit? They are denied and derided, rejected, trampled upon.

All I can say is that we have to drop into some kind of tremendous nothingness, a pit without bottom, so to speak, and from that nothingness call out, "Lord, out of the depths I cry to Thee. Hear the voice of my supplication." (Ps. 130:1–2) But it must be a supplication!

A View From The Mountain of Faith

You climb the mountain because you must, because God is calling you. His voice echoes in your ear: "Friend, come up higher." Because it is he who speaks, you move over stones and rocks and deserts and green pastures. You never know when you will reach the top of the mountain, because it is God's holy mountain and he can make it smaller or larger. But you see that daily you are reaching a place that is higher than the one you left behind.

From that place, you can see the pain of mankind. Not only see it, but share it. Above all other pains in this age of "communication," is the pain of loneliness.

Loneliness walks with everyone. There are bishops who are lonely, priests who are lonely, husbands and wives, too, who are lonely. So are children and teenagers, and those entering adult life. But loneliness is especially etched on the face of old age. Truly, they are the *humiliati*. They are the forgotten ones. From the top of that mountain you look on the world below and cry out to the Lord, like Moses did as he came down from the mountain and saw the golden calf being worshiped by his people.

Yes, loneliness sticks to one, like a postage stamp sticks to an envelope, when golden calves are worshiped. Lie flat on your abdomen and look. Look at the valley and see them worshiping the golden calf. Few indeed are those who abide by the Word of God and live with integrity. Everything is bought and sold. The FBI spends enormous amounts of time today trying to collect what they call "strings." The CIA looks at the world and finds spies and liars everywhere. Nobody speaks the truth anymore. And yet, God is truth.

When God shows you what you do not want to see, you cover your face with your hands. You want to curl up and sleep so as not to see. But sleep wears off, and your eyes are open again.

All of humanity is before you, and you see what the prophets of the Bible saw. You see old women collecting food from garbage cans. You see old men and women dying of loneliness in nursing homes that are mostly interested in collecting their patients' pensions. You see women who have given birth to many children being left alone in their old age by those same children, who only contribute money to their mothers' support, as if money were something that God would accept. They hire nurses and provide things that money can buy. But *they* are not there.

Standing on this rocky mountain, I want to cry out to the world. But will my voice reach people? And if it reaches them, will they hear it? Remember Lazarus and the rich man (Luke 16:19–21). Well, the rich man did not hear. Neither will they today.

Several countries are on the brink of annihilation, not because an enemy is at their doorstep, but because of inflation. And when you go into the core of inflation, my friend, what do you see but greed and selfishness again.

I cannot cry out to everyone; the earth is too big. But I can cry. Do you know what I mean? I can cry. I can cry bitter tears and let them fall on the rocks, which the hearts of men resemble today. Tell me, my friend, do rocks melt? If someone who is in love with God and in love with people cries over the scene that he sees from the heights of the mountain, will the rocks melt?

I do not know. All I know is that somehow, crippled and tired as I am, I must build a house on that rock. It will be the house of God. And those of you who will seek this house will follow the voice of Christ. For to you, too, he will say, "Friend, come up higher."

Fear, craven fear, has gotten hold of people. I feel its breath. It is fetid. What am I to do? How can I, who am nobody, lessen people's fear? In our days of nuclear bombs and of wars and rumors of war, fear, like the serpent of old, crawls up the tree of faith. And wherever it passes, the bark vanishes; the tree stands there naked, seemingly dying.

What am I to do? I am like one pressured on both sides. On one side is people's fear, with its fetid breath coming in waves. People go about their business while the serpent tears away the bark of faith and slithers up and up toward the foliage, which it will devour if it is not stopped. Before the serpent and the tree I stand as one dumb and unable to move. On the other side is God. Have you ever been squeezed in that kind of vise? But, of course, if God calls, one answers. I do. I tell him plainly, humbly, and simply, "Lord, speak; for your servant is listening." (See 1 Sam. 3:10.)

He begins to speak, and he wants me to pass his words on to others, face to face. I am not a prophet. I am, if you want to know, a nobody—just a lay apostle who began apostolic service fifty years ago; that is all. And yet, the strange voice seems to whisper in my ears, "Go, tell them that I love them. Tell them that I want to be loved back, that I came to save everybody. Go, tell them I meant it and I still mean it. Tell them the Good News. Preach it to the fearful ones, to the rich and the poor, to everybody.

"Keep climbing the mountain. You left a house dedicated to me there, as I asked you to. It was built on rock. But now you have to face the fear of people, and it will intensify. This fear will come like a thief in the night and enter into every corner as prices rise and as money loses its value.

"Proclaim that I am God of all nations, that I am a Lover, and that, before me, all fear vanishes. A Lover like myself has power over fears. Faith overcomes all fears. My hands are open. Come, hold them. Learn that I am meek and humble of heart. Learn to be dispossessed of all things except me, my Father, and the Holy Spirit.

"Yes, fear will vanish and rumors of war will quieten down if the world stops being greedy and selfish and interested only in money and wealth. See how everybody is grabbing wealth from everybody. Look at what is happening to the Third World. Look at what the First World is doing to the Third World. Get angry! Stand on the mountain and proclaim the commandments of Yahweh God, and commandments that I brought to earth and gave you. Tell the nations, tell the people, that they must love one another as I have loved them—or perish."

I find myself saying, "I believe. I believe. *Credo*: I believe." True, there are moments when I fear, and other moments when I doubt. But these fears and doubts vanish before the immense tree of faith whose roots are firmly planted in water; for even when the hot season comes, the tree is green. Today our great tragedy is lack of faith. From this mountain I see great lack of faith. I want to close my eyes and I do, but nothing happens. Even through closed eyes I continue to see.

A tragedy envelops me like a dark mantle on the height of that mountain that has no summit, for I see priests leaving the Church from almost every diocese in the world. One by one they turn and walk away.

Do you remember that Christ said to his apostles: "You received without charge, give without charge. Provide yourselves with no gold or silver, not even with a few coppers for your purses, with no haversack for the journey or spare tunic or footwear or a staff"? (Matt. 10: 8–10). He sent them out two by two. What happens today? From the top of this mountain that has no summit, I see many of them turn and walk in the opposite direction from that which Christ indicated.

There are around me huge stones. I sit on one, and I am not ashamed to say that I cry bitter tears. Each tear seems to fall on the stones without making any indentation on them. I cry for priests, but many of their hearts seem to be hard and my tears seem to make no difference.

But then, why should they? I am nobody. I am not important. I am just a woman who cries bitter tears over her beloved priests. Why should it matter to anybody? Of course it doesn't matter. And yet, out of this darkness that seems to envelop the mountain, I hear the whisper of the wind saying, "Keep weeping. I wept, too, before Lazarus' tomb. Then Lazarus rose from the dead because of my tears and because of my prayers to my Father." I know I must continue to weep, and I shall, because Christ wept.

I fell asleep, somewhere between the huge stones that raised their ragged edges to a dark heaven. When I awoke, the wind came and whispered, "Climb." Groggy with sleep and tiredness and with everything that was happening to me, I climbed, sluggishly, holding on to the ragged edges of the enormous stony mountain. Sometimes the rocks seemed to form a stairway, which presented an easy climb . At other times I seemed to be climbing sheer cliffs, holding onto bits of rock that stuck out.

Finally I reached, not the summit of the mountain—it seemed to elude me always—but a sort of plateau that allowed sitting and standing and walking. I looked down. The winds had become rougher, tearing at my clothes and my hair, and they seemed to whisper, "Look. Look below."

I looked, and almost fell off the plateau, for below me, men were killing men. The first thing I saw was blood, blood that flowed freely, all over the world. Crime was rampant in the so–called civilized world, and blood flowed from the deeds of muggers and murderers.

As I kept looking, I realized that from one end of the world to the other, men were in battle array. Oh, not an official battle array like a war. But they were at war. Some were feuding among themselves. Others were trying to get freedom from an oppressor, fighting and being killed. The conquered were in turn killing their conquerors. Thousands were being killed.

Wherever I looked, across immense seas of water or across fantastic and rugged mountains, I saw war: sometimes hidden, sometimes open, but war. For awhile I was like one dead. Then the winds slapped me back into reality, for they were harsh, cold winds that swept across that plateau. They seemed to scream, "Look!" So I looked again.

I saw another war, a war that nobody mentions very much—the war among giants of industry. Not only family farms, but little shops and small businesses were disappearing into the maw of conglomerates of one type or another. I saw this happening not only in the Western world, but even in the East, in Hong Kong, Singapore, Taiwan, South Korea, China, Japan. Conglomerates were swallowing everything that was small, everything that involved real human relations between buyer and seller. All the small disappeared.

Then I saw something more horrible: the conglomerates were getting together and ruling the world. It was no longer a government that ruled a country. It was the conglomerates that ruled most countries. I couldn't look any more. The wind slapped me again and said, "Look!" I looked and became exhausted just by looking.

For I saw yet another war, the war in the minds of men, from where all wars stem. The mind of man was in chaos and turmoil. Just as those wars and those conglomerates created turmoil and chaos all around, so the mind of man became, everywhere, chaotic. It did not know what to do.

For a moment I thought I was seeing a puppet show, for men, women, and children seemed to go around and around in a sort of macabre dance, to a music I couldn't hear. Each person was alone in this endless motion. But then I saw how man began facing himself, and asking, "Where am I going?" Soon he was asking, "Where are *we* going?"

For all this chaos had been created by a system that ceased to be able to function, by governments that were powerless against each other and also powerless in their own countries.

People were seeking a road or a path, a way, and not finding it. All around them was a desert filled with cactuses and tumbleweeds and other prickly things that lifted their huge arms to heaven. But there was no road. So I cried out, "Where are the highways? Where are the byways? Where are the little roads?" No one answered. The wind lashed at me and howled, as winds do on high places: "Look and understand." I looked, and tried to understand.

Man had two roads left to him. One was Marxism, the other, capitalism. There was really nothing in between. I stood on my plateau and let the winds almost tear me apart, because what I saw pushed me as close to despair as a person like me could be—a person who has been in love with God since she was six years old, and whose faith had, so far, survived all that life had dished out to her.

Then I realized that my faith was unimpaired, that large, strong roots were growing into my plateau, entering into the stony ground, and somehow breaking it into small pieces. The tree of my faith was growing and growing, and its branches sheltered me from the rough winds.

I saw, from the shade cast by my tree of faith, a third path, the path of Christ: simple, direct, not a highway or a throughway, but just a little country path. That is the path man should take, because there he will find peace. I understood, without understanding, that man rejected this path because of pride, greed, and desire for possessions. Men also fought over what they called "ideals."

Yes, I saw this clearly from the shade of my tree of faith. And I knew that someday, maybe tomorrow or the day after, maybe many hundreds of years from now, men will discover the little paths, the country roads that lead to faith, to love, to hope; but above all, to brotherhood, which is the fruit of that tree. Then all will be one. Frontiers will drop away like an old worn coat. Then man will go toward God in brotherhood. Christ, the Father, and the Holy Spirit will guide us all. Then the face of God will be evident in the faces of all men.

IV

Repent!

Once upon a time God, after having been very angry with the Jewish people, in his mercy and kindness stopped being angry and said, "Come, let us talk things over" (Isa. 1:18). A very strange part of the Old Testament, this so-called anger of God and then his invitation to sit down and talk things over. If only it could happen now!

But, of course, in order for it to happen, several things are necessary. First, people must believe in God; otherwise how can they "sit down with him and talk things over"? Secondly, those who believe must stop being angry against God. For in our days there is less anger of God toward his beloved people than there is anger in the heart of man against God.

I continue climbing my mountain. But this time, somehow, I am in very lovely green pastures. How they grew on top of those terrible stones and rocks and precipices that I was climbing so fearfully yesterday, I don't know. But the air is clear, the pastures green. And all around me, the winds bring me the mercy of God, his forgiveness, his tenderness, his love.

Sitting on a knoll, I try to absorb the whole thing. It is hard to absorb because of its strange peace. The winds bring me the words of Christ: "Peace I bequeath to you, my own peace I give you, a peace the world cannot give, this is my gift to you" (John 14:27). And as I sit there, suddenly, in the midst of a green field, a cross begins to grow. Where did it come from? There is no wood around there, but the cross grew. Slowly the upright beam became ten feet high, and the transverse beam grew from the very heart of it. I drew back.

The knoll was small. I tried to find some place where I could hide or at least find a wall to lean my back against. I found nothing, but noticed that the cross grew on a larger knoll. I realized that I was sitting before Golgotha, for the cross on which Christ was crucified was also on a knoll.

I contemplated what was happening, and could only kneel and adore the cross. Then out of the mountains a wind came. It picked me up and threw me down, like hurricanes do, and shouted, "Speak! Speak!"

Lying flat on the green earth, overshadowed by this cross that grew so strangely, I asked, "What shall I say?" I thought to say that the Lord is calling everyone to sit down and talk things over. But they don't believe in God! The majority don't. They don't want to sit down with him. They don't want to listen to what he has to say.

Still, I opened my mouth and, like a torrent, words spilled out. It occurred to me that if a big chalice had been held there to catch my words, it would have been overflowing.

I knew that I was not myself. The winds spoke for me. I remembered Christ's words: "When they hand you over, do not worry about how to speak or what to say. What you are to say will be given to you when the time comes, because it is not you who will be speaking; the

Spirit of your Father will be speaking in you" (Matt. 10: 19–20).

I was awed that out of my mouth came the words of Christ, for that is the way it was. I wasn't thinking. I felt almost dead, and yet I was standing straight, unafraid. I was speaking these words from the mountain, and they went across the world.

Yes, all heard what I had to say, because it wasn't I who was speaking. My tongue and my mouth were used to tell the world what had to happen. I was saying, "Repent! Repent! Repent!" until I was tired of the word. But I had to repeat it again and again.

Then I said, "Repent and make peace with one another or you shall all perish in the great fire that is forthcoming. Can't you see? Are you blind? Are you deaf? Repent. This is the time of repentance. This is the time of asking forgiveness of God and then of your neighbor. For we have all sinned against him and against our neighbor. We still have time to repent, to cry out to God, *"Kyrie eleison! Christe eleison!* O Lord, have mercy on me, a sinner."

We still have time to turn to our brother and be reconciled with him before we bring our offering to the altar. But there is little time. The invitation of God to come and talk things over will not last forever, because we shall be like the captives of Babylon. We shall be annihilated, and those of us who will not die the merciful death of the body will cry out for forgiveness, for repentance. And do you know something? God will hear us. Even if it is at the last hour.

The terrain became flat, with no trees. Some grass sprouted here and there, as if it did not want to but had to. The whole place turned drab and gray. Its dull monotony brought depression to my heart.

I looked around. The place was filled with people going about their business, selling and buying before their own temples. There was practically no breeze. I stood in the midst of all those people, being elbowed and pushed around, knowing I was called to preach the Gospel with my life. But in these dull surroundings, among these drab sellers and buyers, I didn't feel like opening my mouth.

Then a small wind touched me. It was very soft. It almost didn't seem as if it was a wind at all. Yet it entered my heart and repeated to me the message that I knew already: "Speak. Tell the Good News that is preached to the poor." I shook myself. I shook myself like dogs shake themselves when they come out of the water. It seemed incomprehensible that I was to talk to these buyers and sellers, to these people who crowded this desolate terrain filled with buildings devoted to selling and buying.

I hesitated. It was so difficult, so terribly difficult. But I knew that I had to do it. There was no promontory of any kind, no hill, no boulders or stones that I could stand on. There was nothing but this drab, gray terrain criss-crossed with sidewalks and people rushing around like mad, buying and selling.

There was a sort of children's playground there, though there were no children. I walked toward it, saw a bench and climbed on it. To proclaim the Good News you had to have a little height, so I thought.

I spoke of the love of God, of his tenderness, his mercy, his love for us. I spoke of faith, of hope, of love. I spoke of the miracles he had performed. I spoke of the Old Testament and blended the New into the Old. I brought the New Testament in all its purity and simplicity before everybody. I spoke, because thoughts came to me, unbidden, as if someone filled my mind with what to say. I remembered that God said he would speak in us in times of need and difficulty.

Do you know something? My voice, which was fairly powerful, seemed to be absorbed into a huge ball of cotton like that used in hospitals, and it died there. For I was talking to people who were not listening. They were utterly and completely indifferent to what I said. They passed me by without even turning their heads.

They didn't want to argue anything. No theological or philosophical or other kinds of verities penetrated their hearts. Nothing. They were like a herd of sheep without a shepherd. They moved around, interested only in the buying and the selling, nothing else. It seemed that they could not even remember what was on television. I heard one man say to his wife as they were passing me by, "Oh, I don't remember what the story was. I was too busy figuring out that big deal ahead of me."

Yes, that was all they were interested in: "deals". Honest deals, dishonest deals—it didn't matter, so long as they made their money. That was all. And when they had made their money, they came to their families or their wives or their friends and they laid down a cheque and said, "See? I made almost a hundred percent profit on that deal."

At night I could see electric signs everywhere, inviting people to have a drink or some fun or whatever, or advertising a restaurant. I was getting dizzy from all those neon lights. They looked to me like lights from hell.

My voice got hoarse as I stood alone speaking from the childlike platform. Still I kept proclaiming: "Christ asked us to love one another as he loved us. Think about that." But nobody did. Not a soul. I was standing among the indifferent ones, among ones who thought only of money. They were selling and buying, not only in front of temples, but everywhere! One can speak to the blind, but can one speak to the deaf?

I felt scalding tears fall on my face, and called out to God, "Lord, have mercy!" A quiet and peace–filled voice answered, "That is who I am—the Lord of mercy."

At that I knew not where I was, other than on God's mountain, the summit of which I never quite reach. Somehow I seemed suspended over a tremendous precipice that opened on the whole world. I was lying flat on my abdomen and looking down, and insanity seemed to take hold of me. Then cold, brusque winds came up and blew away my thoughts, and I didn't feel insane any more. I knew that I must preach the Word of God.

But was this impossible? For at the bottom of the mountain people seemed to be struggling in some kind of battle. Strangely, there were no tanks or men armed with guns, nothing resembling either a trench war or a *blitzkrieg*. There was no Maginot line. But from the mountain heights, people looked as if they were ants scurrying, crowding the bridges, crowding the waters. They were swimming across the Hudson River, swimming across the East River; they were crossing across any river they could find in the U.S.A. Bridges were collapsing under the weight of overloaded cars.

People were trying to run from the atomic bomb, which was whispered to be coming. I remembered a time, not long after Hiroshima, when the government devised plans for evacuating the people of New York. They came to the conclusion that it was impossible, that ten million people, considering Brooklyn and Manhattan together, could not all be evacuated. Some would have to die.

The winds said, "Speak. Speak." So I lifted my voice and called out, "Stop it! Stop it! Don't do it! Don't activate your arms, made for the destruction of the world. You want to bomb Russia and Russia wants to bomb you. Don't do it! Don't do it!

"Look! In the midst of your airplanes, missiles, and submarines stands an enormous cross. It is as big as the sky. It loses itself in the universe. The transverse beam touches unknown areas. It comes from the hearts of men. See how it goes up and up and up, to the feet of God the Father; how its shadow falls on the whole world. Don't do it! Don't do what you want to do! Don't annihilate! Don't kill! It is against the commandments of God—the loving God who died for us. Don't do it! Remember that he said, 'I am meek and humble of heart.' Follow him. Be meek, be humble, forgive, repent. Repent! *Repent!*"

My voice rose like thunder, but no one paid any attention to it. Missiles were there, ready to fire. And fire they did. Still lying flat and looking down, I could see the whole world. I saw something very unusual, both in the Third World and in the First World. Fighting had almost stopped and people were on their knees, praying.

The United States had destroyed Moscow and Leningrad and a lot of places where missiles were being made in Siberia. The enormous mass of the U.S.S.R., which I call Russia, took on its breast the full force of the missiles, shivered, and suffered much destruction.

Then came the retaliation. For the U.S. had not known where, in the depths of the earth, more missiles had been hidden. New York, Chicago, Washington, and San Francisco were targets. Huge buildings, the immense work of men's hands that had resembled the Tower of Babel, fell like a house of cards made by a child. In falling, they killed millions.

Lying flat on the rocks, I saw it all and wept, for I loved. You weep for one you love who seems to die. The wind came at me, still cold, but more gently, and out of the wind came a voice: "Now they have seen what their pride and arrogance have done. Pray that they will return to my Father."

A fog enveloped me, a warm fog which held me tight. I rested in it, and didn't want to look at anybody or anything. But out of nowhere came a breeze that whispered in my ear, "Speak. Speak." So I had to proclaim the Good News through the fog.

I began to tell people that God came to save us, that he lived among us, that he was crucified for us, that he loved us beyond all our imagination, beyond all that we ever thought love was like. I quoted again and again the Beatitudes, the commandments of love that Jesus Christ left us before he ascended to his Father.

All my words came back to me, right through the fog. I took a deep breath, opened my eyes and looked.

Beyond the fog I could see the hearts of men. I saw with horror and fear that they were buried under gold, silver, and all kinds of valuable things. They didn't understand that they were slowly being suffocated to death. For the gold and silver were heavy, and were literally crushing their owners. But these people stretched out their hands and cried out, "More gold! More silver! More everything!"

Here was the ultimate sin, the sin of greed, selfishness, and pride. What could I do against it, except to cry out into the fog that they should stop while they were still alive. But that seemed impossible for them to understand. They were selling themselves with that gold and that silver. On the stock exchanges of the world they were buying and selling gold or its paper equivalent, stocks, which would give them, so they thought, happiness.

"Stop," I cried out to them again, "Wake up! Repent! Come to God! There is still time!" But my voice was muffled by the fog. Loud as it might have seemed to me, it didn't reach anyone, or perhaps only a few.

I understood at that moment, with a sort of lightning understanding, why we of Madonna House* exist. We exist to show the face of Christ through all the fogs, through all the storms, through all the rains and hurricanes. We exist, if need be, to be martyred. Because only martyrs, bloodied martyrs, can penetrate that fog, can with their two hands lift off from people the weight of gold and silver that was suffocating them.

Again I looked and saw the frenzied desires of men. They were all wrapped in greed and selfishness. Heads of states took away the bread from the mouth of the poor. I began to shake uncontrollably, because I saw also the anger of God.

I knew that I had to enter that anger, that I had to plead for these people, that I had to cry out to God to

---

*Madonna House is the Catholic community founded by the author.

forgive them, as Moses did when he came down from the mountain and saw the golden calf. So I entered the anger of God, knelt at his feet, and implored him to forgive people's sins of greed and selfishness and especially of unrepentance, which were leading them to war.

Just as I fell totally exhausted at the feet of God the Father crying, "Abba! Abba! Be merciful! Be merciful to us sinners!" I heard a gentle voice say, "My Father and I and the Holy Spirit are always merciful, always forgiving. Remember that."

Preach the Good News!

The day is clear. The sun is shining. Down below there are beautiful shadows. People seem to walk in peace; at least from above they look peaceful. I sit on a piece of petrified wood, the stump of a tree that must have grown thousands of years ago. One could count the rings inside it, which tell its age when it was felled. As I look at the whole world from my old tree stump, everybody appears to be hurrying, to be running around in circles, and I wonder why.

In fact those who are running want to push away those who run by their side. It is like a rat race. I can hardly believe my eyes, for they also want to get on top of the others' shoulders. Now they form a pyramid. Each person wants to be on top of somebody else's shoulders.

Then I understand: they are competing. Competition literally kills family, friends, anybody; but above all, it kills love. We can't love and also compete with one another.

As I look I begin to understand that unless they reach the top of their pyramids, people consider themselves to be rejected, to be the offal of society, to be nobodies. They can't stand being nobodies. Thus the strange running around in ever bigger circles, the strange leap that a man or a woman takes onto the shoulders of somebody else, onto the pyramid. What are they trying to do with that pyramid? Reach heaven?

The strangest thing of all, as I sit on my stump and look, is that I hear laughter. I hear demonic laughter, and I know that it comes from hell. What can I do? I search my heart. Something has to be done. People can't live like this.

Then from my tree trunk on God's mountain I notice that the pyramid seems to become inverted—the pyramid formed by people running and jumping on somebody else's shoulders. I get up to look; the pyramid is in fact inverted. And those who were on the top are going down, down, down, into the depths of hell. I cry out to God, "What can I do?" The wind that blows on the holy mountain says, "Preach the Good News.

"Understand what you are seeing. Because only people like yourself whom God has specially selected can re-invert that pyramid, can break it up. Yes, God has selected a few of you to do just this. So get up now on your tree stump, and preach! Tell them that happiness is found in the heart of God. Tell them that happiness is humility and meekness, love and hope. Tell of the tree of faith. Stand up and tell them."

So I stand up and tell them. The strange part of this whole thing is that with my weak little voice I seem able to reach the ends of the earth! I cannot understand that.

In fact I don't understand anything. Here I am, in various places on the holy mountain, and I do things because the wind tells me to. The wind is always the Holy Spirit. I am just obedient. The wind brings me this word from Jesus Christ: "I was obedient to my Father unto death, and so are you."

Sitting at the very edge of the pine forest in the eventide, I look down. Suddenly I am not there at all! I am where my heart has always been; I am with the poor. A love, a joy, a simple, childlike joy fills my heart and I tell myself, "I am descending the holy mountain to go to the poor."

But the wind that is always around the holy mountain tells me, "No. They are coming to you." Immediately I think, "If they are coming to me, I must make a feast. I must feed them and clothe them and help them in some way."

I begin to beg, for I have no money. To give them a good meal, to clothe them, to make them happy, I must beg money. It is not easy; I tried, when I accepted poverty totally. The poor were never given any eggs. Bread, yes, and tea or coffee. Maybe some soup. But eggs, no. That was for the rich. Still, I went around begging.

People sometimes ask me why we in Madonna House are beggars. I answer very simply, "Beggars are the ambassadors of God." Peter Maurin, who helped Dorothy Day begin the *Catholic Worker*, and who probably will be canonized, put that in his book.

As I stop in the darkening twilight of the fir trees, I begin to understand how beautiful begging is, begging for somebody else. That is what St. Francis did. Yes, St. Francis was a beggar. He gives me courage to knock at the door of people and to have those doors slammed in my face sometimes. That is all right. Then I truly learn to be meek and humble.

But what has begging to do with what we are going through these days? It is because people do not want to share their wealth, be it a dollar or a million, that we are on the eve of a catastrophe. When people do not share their wealth, what else remains but a catastrophe? Begging reminds people that God calls us to share what we have with those in need.

Once upon a time Christ said, "I was hungry and you never gave me food; I was thirsty and you never gave me anything to drink; I was a stranger and you never made me welcome, naked and you never clothed me, sick and in prison and you never visited me" (Matt. 25:42–43). All of us who haven't done those things shall cry out, "When have we not done these things to you?" And Christ, looking us straight in the eye, will say to us, "Insofar as you neglected to do this to one of the least, you neglected to do it me" (Matt. 25:45).

People of the world, listen! Do listen! An immense abyss is opening before us, and we are going into it as if called by some Lorelei on the Rhine. Don't you understand, don't we all understand, that we must begin to share? We must! It is not a question of tithing. It is a question of sharing, because unless we share, we will become atomic dust. That is all we will be. There is still time.

Listen! Awake! Stop! Stop trying to be a millionaire. Everybody wants to be a millionaire these days. Become poor. Become a beggar. Because, if you remember, Christ always looked for the humble ones, the ones that were rejected by society—the prostitutes, the thieves, the tax collectors, the crooks. He went to have supper with them. When the big shots of his time, whoever they were, called the attention of the apostles to the behavior of their leader, Christ answered for the apostles, "It is not the healthy who need the doctor, but the sick" (Matt. 9:12).

I project my voice across the world, which doesn't seem to listen. I want to be a beggar; I *am* a beggar. The winds say, "Yes, you are begging because you love people. You are begging to give them hope, to give them faith." Christ says, "I am also a beggar. I beg for the love of people's hearts. So, give me your hand. We both are beggars for the most precious things in life."

At that point I was passing through a town of many thousands of people. But the whole place was drab and gray and unappealing; it gave the impression of indifference. Shop windows were not washed. The pavement was cracked. I felt that the quicker I passed through this town the better; the journey from one end of it to the other dragged on. A pall of indifference, of sadness almost, came over me as I was leaving this town behind.

Yes, it was that kind of place. You fell asleep, or almost so, at the wheel of the car, or if you were traveling by horses it seemed as if you let the reins go. An indifference, the likes of which I had never experienced, took hold of me. I frankly did not even care if God existed or didn't exist. I wasn't going to open my mouth and preach what he called the "Good Tidings." No.

Completely indifferent to everything, I still knew one thing, that I was climbing, eternally climbing, the mountain of the Lord. Have you ever climbed the mountain of the Lord almost unwillingly? Indifferently? The wind blew around me as it always did, but I had no response to it. I was weary beyond all weariness. I couldn't remember a day when I was that weary.

It seemed that the task the Lord had given me to do, namely, to preach his Gospel as clearly as I could, was finished. I didn't want to preach. I just wanted to sleep, to escape, to go away some place where I wouldn't be bothered with so many people.

But I had to go on. I recalled once speaking to a crowd of 33,000 people. They surrounded me, almost crushed me against an unseen wall, wanting more words from me. Have you ever encountered people who believed you had gifts that you knew you didn't have? They wanted me to keep talking. I looked into my heart, and there was nothing there but desire to get out of that mob. I promised myself never to talk to so many people again.

I was tired beyond my own understanding, and, I think, beyond the understanding of many. I knew that the people chosen by God to bring his message to the world were always tired. But I did not know *how* tired.

Did you ever feel this numbing, crushing tiredness that takes hold of you and seems to crush you into powder? There you are, lying on the road, a little handful of powder. The words of Ash Wednesday came back to me: "Remember, man, that thou art dust, and unto dust thou shalt return." That is exactly how I felt.

The wind around me became harsher, more powerful. It wasn't whispering any more; its voice was simple and clear. It kept urging, "Arise. Go! Preach! Tell the Good Tidings to the poor. And remember that everybody is poor."

As I sat there on a fire hydrant I remembered that I was the poorest of all. Yes, I sat on a hydrant and realized my utter poverty. Of myself, I could do nothing, neither arise, nor go any place, nor speak about the Glad Tidings. I was numb and dumb, seemingly incapable of speech. Yes, I was weary beyond all weariness.

Then on all sides voices began calling to me. They were moving toward me, and there were tears in these voices as they said, "Speak to us! Speak to us about the Glad Tidings, about his love for us. We are hungry. We are thirsty. We are in a desert. You have water. You have food. Share it with us. Speak to us!" It seemed as if this vast cry penetrated my tiredness, unloosed my dumbness, and opened my ears, as Christ did when, in healing the deaf man, he said, "*Ephpheta!* — Be opened!" (Mark 7:34).

Yes, I was again able to talk, to listen, to answer. Through the gray curtain of tiredness, I spoke. Once more I told them, in a clear voice, how much God loves us, how he died for us, how he is in our midst now, and for all time. I said this, and much more. When I finished, I fainted, and slid down the hydrant.

As I regained consciousness I got on my knees and cried out, "Lord, have mercy." That was all I could say; my voice seemed to be coming out of subconscious depths. But I kept repeating this chant that welled up from my heart: "Lord, have mercy; Lord, have mercy; Lord, have mercy." And from the winds came the familiar voice, "Now you know how tired I was when I hung on the Cross. But love overcomes tiredness. Mine did."

Lord, Have Mercy!

It is raining, and foggy, and the stones are slippery. I'm tired and I don't want to go up this strange mountain any more. I move forward a little, then slip back.

Suddenly anger, like a raging fire, envelops me. I want to cry out to God, when I consider all the poor and miserable people who are trying to eke out a meager living in the richest countries of the world: Canada, America, Western Europe. This is to say nothing of the poor and destitute in other countries where millions don't have enough to eat. We are face to face with a lack of charity, of compassion.

I call out to God, "Lord, I want to cry. For I see, and seeing brings forth tears. But the majority do not weep. How are they going to appear before you, Lord? Have mercy on us, have mercy on us, have mercy on us. I cannot believe that you will abandon the poor, and yet there they are, seemingly utterly abandoned.

"Lord, hear my plea. I am not crying for myself but only for others. I am crying out of the depths. Maybe my voice cannot reach you. But with the last breath of my body I must cry out to you: *Kyrie eleison! Christe eleison! Kyrie eleison!* Lord, have mercy! Christ, have mercy!

Gospodi pomiluj mne greshnya! Lord, have mercy! *Jesus, prends pitie!*

Out of the wind that always seems to surround me I hear a voice: "Be at peace. I am with you unto the end of time. What is happening I cannot control because I have given people freedom, and people are exercising their freedom. But I am with you always unto the end of time."

My mind tried to figure out where I was, for now the terrain became flat again. And it stunk! This was the first time that such odors had come to me on the holy mountain. Plateaus in mountains are often associated with the scent of flowers or pine, or some other pleasant smell. This one wasn't.

I looked around and realized that I was where my heart has been for the last fifty years: in what people call the slums, or depressed areas. Yes, I was in the midst of a slum.

One side seemed to be reserved for the minority groups of which I am a member, the Slavs: Russians, Yugoslavs, Ukrainians. On the other side of this slum lived Latinos: South Americans, Puerto Ricans, Chicanos. I was surrounded with wonderful, friendly people who were, as a social worker would put it, terribly underprivileged.

I was happy to be again amongst the *humiliati*: the dispossessed, the poor, the disliked. Christ was one of the *humiliati*. He was like the man besieged by robbers. He was crucified alongside criminals, like a slave. He was a poor man like Lazarus, trying to find some crumbs from a rich man's table.

I knelt down amid the garbage cans, which were overflowing, and kissed the earth, because I was on holy ground. I was in the midst of the *humiliati*, the rejected ones, the forgotten ones, the ones nobody wants to take care of, except perhaps through government "welfare."

Memories from my years in the slums started coming back to me, as if they were pictures in a movie. I saw elderly fathers and mothers huddled in their corners. Sometimes they had a rocking chair; sometimes they didn't. I visited my neighbors in the slums very often, not because I was good, but because I knew that Jesus Christ was in their midst. In fact he *was* the poor. I considered it a great honor to be in their midst.

There was little Miss O'Reilly, who was all twisted up with arthritis and couldn't go anywhere. I used to do her shopping. If she had been eating only what government 'relief' was giving her in those days, she would probably have starved to death. So our Friendship House added something from what little they had to look after Miss O'Reilly.

Then there was another woman, whose last name I forgot—the poor don't often use their last names. She was called Margaret. She had a son about five, and she was dying from cancer. Her little son was sent to an orphanage. They treated him passably well, but what is an orphanage compared to a mother's love?

While serving in Friendship House, in the slums of Harlem, I myself got sick once, with strep throat. Having a high fever, I was taken to the hospital but they refused to treat me because, you see, I didn't have any health insurance, I wasn't on government "relief," and I had no visible means of support. (It was by begging that we lived and served the poor.) So, in short, I didn't qualify for medical care. I was brought back home.

Never will I forget the gentleness and kindness of all our black neighbors, who rallied to care for me. Someone was always there to give me a drink of water or to put cold compresses on my burning head—to do what they could, with loving concern.

Memories come of a woman who had just moved into an unheated house in the city of Toronto; this was in the early thirties when there were plenty of empty houses. It was only two blocks from where I lived. Somebody told me about her and I went to her. The picture I saw is etched in my mind forever. Three little children in their coats were huddled near their mother, who was giving suck to a baby who was dead.

I could go on indefinitely, telling stories of what I have seen. Perhaps it is better not to tell them. Yet I must tell them in order to wake up sluggish, laggard souls and hearts. I cry out, "Come, change your way of life, your style of life. Share! Share what you have! If you have a dollar, share it. Give twenty-five cents to the poor and keep seventy-five cents for yourself. Awake! Do something. Act as if you are Christians, as if you belong to Christ!"

The poor who were suffering were constantly before my mind's eyes. All of them—the Chicanos, blacks, other minority groups—all became Christ, the powerful, beautiful Christ. I looked at him and he at me. Then the winds came again, bringing his words to me: "I am still in their midst, poor with the poor, poor with the rich. The greedy, the selfish, the indifferent are bringing disaster upon themselves. Pray that your tears do not fall on the stony hearts of men who close their doors to anyone but themselves."

Wars and Rumors of Wars

An immense peace surrounded the Lord's mountain and it seemed as if countless choirs were singing. Yet as I looked down from this very high mountain I saw the world in turmoil. There was much terrorism and war. I saw heads of governments unable to cope with the people. Where there was a modicum of democracy, it seemed the people did not trust their government.

Standing with my back against a rock, I called to all the nations of the world, especially the Christian ones, to stop killing each other, to stop taking hostages, to stop terrorizing people and being terrorists themselves. For a terrorist is someone who hates. God never hates.

I cried out to God for those who are being held hostages in various countries. I wept with those who are related to them. I knew that Christ weeps too, and so does his Mother, Our Lady.

As powerfully as I could, I cried out to everyone, "Look! Christ loved us so much. He loved us enough to become man. He loved us enough to die on the Cross. He loved us. Awake! Love him back. The moment you will love him back, that very moment peace will come. Peace will come into your hearts and wars will cease.

"Open your hearts and your souls to his words. Don't let him stand there in front of your doors, without letting him in. Peace will not come to this earth if you continue to be deaf to his words." When my voice gave in, I fell down and wept. I wept for him who loved us so much, and for all of us who did not love him.

Around me thousands of angry people were screaming and yelling and shaking their fists at God. I wanted to run, to close my eyes and ears so as not to hear. But, surrounded as I was by crowds of angry people from all over the world, I got up again, stood on a promontory and spoke to them.

"Yes, I know. I spent fifty years in the Harlems of America, in the slums of Toronto, and in rural slums, serving the poor. I know why you scream and yell and raise your fists to God. But stop, and understand.

"It isn't God who created the conditions under which you are living and working. It is the rich, the powerful, who have reduced you to the poverty that you are in. In spite of that, you don't have to hate them. Love them. Get organized and confront them, but not with revolvers or grenades. No; confront them with love and forgiveness."

Then I lost track of where I was again. Before my mind's eye passed, as in a movie, a series of pictures. There were all the great kingdoms of antiquity. I saw Babylon and Egypt and Rome, with Attila and the barbarians overrunning it. I saw Alexander the Great plundering the world. I saw Genghis Khan. I kept seeing ruins of kingdoms and empires, ruin upon ruin upon ruin.

Then came a strong British Empire. Strange, wasn't it, that from my stone on the mountain of the Lord, I saw water all over, and a little island of no account? Suddenly, out of that island came war, just like the wars that had been before.

After that the island somehow vanished. Did it vanish in the water or did it just vanish? I couldn't tell. So many countries have vanished in various places. I knew my own country, Russia, had been conquered for four hundred years by the Tartars. They also had created an empire. But the English, they had a civilized empire.

Next came America, after World War I and World War II. They were a bountiful people who gave things to everybody, but also took something from everybody.

Abruptly the scene changed, and I seemed to be among warring Muslims. I thought that Muslims were merciful to their enemies, but then I get mixed up. Next the scene became Afghanistan. The mountains were very rough and I was trudging with my arthritic knees behind covered wagons like those I had trudged behind when I was young.

Then almost instantly I found myself between the P.L.O. and the Jews. Everywhere I looked, there was war going on, now hidden, now open, now diplomatic, now direct—people killing each other.

These scenes were very mixed up, yet the strangest thing about them was that they were all practically the same. Clothing was different, the colors of people's skin were different. But the mobs killing one another all seemed alike.

Have you ever been in a mob, and experienced what it does to you? I have. Once when I was in Russia, a mob was in charge, and when mobs are in charge, nobody is in charge. I have heard both Lenin and Hitler speak. Yes, I did. In one ear I can still hear the mellifluous, powerful voice of Lenin, and in the other, the thin, hysterical, but fascinating and hypnotic voice of Hitler. For I was pushed against a wall when I was in Germany and happened to hear Hitler speak.

Mobs—their shouts penetrate your head like nails or thorns. You lose all sense of where you are and what is happening. Whole centuries can pass before your eyes, and all that they bring to your feet is war. War and mobs.

I am trying to climb the mountain of the Lord, but I am not getting very far, because I have been bowed down by a weight bigger than myself. There is no use trying to fool myself or anybody else. If I am supposed to preach the Gospel—and for this I was born—then I have only tears to give people. Because, you see, tears, as Russians say, wash away your own sins and the sin of mankind.

Are you ready to weep? Well, if you are, then the Lord be praised. But so many of you are not ready to weep. So many of you make a mockery of Jesus Christ. So many of you don't believe in him. And yet, notwithstanding all the mockery and unbelief, you are eternally seeking him; you are searchers of God who don't want to find him.

How shall I call you forth from the den of misery in which you have pushed yourself? You are afraid, arrogant, greedy, feeling rejected and lonely, notwithstanding all the gadgets. What more can I say to you? You have the key to the door of Christ's heart. All you have to do is put the key into the lock and open it, and you will be at peace. And peace will come to the world.

But nobody wants to listen, or very few do. Nations hate nations and people hate people. It may seem as if there is no way out, but there is always a way out. The way out is the love of God, the mercy of God, the kindness of God, and above all, the faith that he has put into our hearts.

Is there compassion in us? Are we ready to help the other fellow, even at our expense? Or don't we care the least bit about the poor, the forgotten, the *humiliati?* Moses told Pharaoh what would happen to him if he balked the will of Yahweh. And it came to pass. Well, this is very much the time of our balking. We use our brains and science and all kinds of things to avert inflations and recessions. But one thing we don't do is go on our knees and implore God to have mercy on us. That is what we should do! Why don't we?

The wind keeps saying to me, "Go on preaching. I know your voice is rusty. I know you are tired. But, Catherine, I was tired and my voice was very rusty when I spoke to John and to my Mother from the cross. Crucified people talk with rusty voices. Have no fear. I am with you unto the end of time."

The Cross and The Resurrection

The summit of the mountain is still out of reach. There are black, dark clouds covering it, but no rain. Yet for some reason the stones are slippery, and I have a hard time climbing them.

I look down and am surprised to see a man on a donkey entering some city, and children throwing palm leaves at the donkey's feet. But this lasts only a moment. Then I see a mob pulling and tearing the clothes off that man, laughing at him, jeering at him. He is crowned with thorns, and they nail him to a cross.

The wind becomes like a hurricane. It says clearly, "This is the moment to preach his Gospel. Today is Good Friday, the day when Christ died. Look at him. He is crucified, he is dying. His love is spilling at your feet.

"See how his blood drips from his body. He is naked—the Jews and the Romans didn't have any puritanical ideas about nakedness. He is naked and bruised and bleeding from his wounds.

"Are you going to be silent? Aren't you going to open your mouth? Aren't you going to proclaim to the world the love of God for men? Aren't you going to give men the cup of reconciliation? That is what he came for.

Speak now of Christ reconciling sinful 'Adam' to God, of Christ reconciling humanity and God. Speak now.

"But in order to speak the way he wants you to, you must be crucified on the other side of that cross. Then you will speak. You won't say much. Two crucified people don't speak easily. But what they say remains in the hearts of men."

Taking it to be the Holy Spirit speaking to me, I say, "Lord, I am very tired. I have preached the Gospel for fifty years. There is such a pain in my heart that I don't think I can utter a word, let alone preach to anybody. Isn't it time for me to rest?"

The wind becomes very soft, and a voice comes from the wind saying, "I have given you length of days that you might preach my Good News, because so few do. Open your mouth and preach my Gospel until I tell you to come home."

Looking around, I behold the whole world. It is deeply imbedded through my eyes into my brain, my heart, my soul. The wind is mournfully urging me, "You have only one thing to do, in season and out of season, night and day: you must cry out, across the whole world, Christ's love for all.

"Your voice seems to you to be small, unheard, inspiring no one; you know nothing of what God has wrought in you. You share Christ's pain; the cross is heavy. But God has chosen you to preach, even though the cross crushes you into the dust of the road.

"Open your mouth and speak, even if the ascent to Golgotha, which is part of the mountain of the Lord, is hard on you. If you fall down and hit your face against stones, don't stop! Speak to them. Call them. Implore them. As you lie there flat and bruised, call people to love

God, so that they might have peace, joy, love and hope, and so that all may stand, lean, or lie under the shadow of the tree of faith. Open your mouth and speak!"

Strength comes to me from somewhere. I straighten up a little and address the people, speaking to them from my innermost heart. "People of God, listen. You hear the thunder and see the lightning. The night is dark. But God is with us. He said so. He will be with us to the end of time.

"People of God, whose head is Christ, people of God who are his Mystical Body, his Bride—listen, listen! There is so little time. Don't you see the signs of the mercy of God?"

"This is the time for reconciliation. Soon there will be the great reconciliation of God and man. The world is about to remember that God died on a Cross, a Cross so huge that it embraces the whole world. This is the hour of reconciliation, of forgiveness. Do you wish to hate? Deep down in your soul, in your heart, you do not. Why don't you go deep into your heart? For there you shall meet Christ.

"You doubt. Don't doubt. Listen to his voice: 'Come to me, all you who labor and are overburdened, and I will give you rest' (Matt. 11:28). He will refresh you and you will be a new people. All of you, whoever you are—Jews, Muslims, Gentiles, Catholics, Protestants—you will be a new people. You will be a people that loves one another. Hear the wind. Be still. Through it Christ says to you, 'For this I came to earth, that you may forgive each other and love each other. That will bring the Kingdom of God onto earth. Behold, I am with you unto the end of time. I am with all my children, the heirs of my Father.'"

Now the peace of the mountain envelops me. I know that God is indeed in our midst, in the midst of all. He has taken human form for love of us.

Then I see Love fall upon the mountain. The night suddenly glows with a tremendous light. From the summit of the mountain arises a cross, and spontaneously I cry out, "See how much he loves us. He died on it." Then the cross disappears.

From the summit of the mountain the Lord comes, dressed as an ordinary person. As he approaches, love comes from his heart, like a sea of waves, to the heart of every man, woman, and child. He seems to embrace each one. His descent is luminous, full of love and peace and joy; he is happy to be with us again. At his descent I hear a chant in many languages: "Christ is risen! Truly he is risen!" The great joy of Easter overcomes me.

It is a lovely spring day. The apple blossoms are perfuming everything with their fragrance. Out in the forest a thousand little trees, whose existence one would hardly suspect, are also blossoming and sending their perfume across a renewed world.

Thoughts of the resurrection crowd my heart. I am still walking up toward the summit of God's mountain, but the walking is easy. Spring has placed a green carpet under my feet. Yes, everything is coming to life, and my heart is happy because, strange as it might seem, some people are listening.

Everything is alive. Everything is beautiful. But above all, the hearts of men are beautiful. They listen to the words of God. Yes, it seems strange, because I am not used to men listening. I am used to pouring my tears over their stony hearts. But there are, at the moment, no stony hearts. The ones I see, the ones I hear, are listening.

Yes, people are listening. They are not only listening, they are incarnating the words they hear. Now Christ's Gospel is being lived, without compromise.

I sing out, "How beautiful are your miracles, Lord! For this indeed is a miracle—that man, pausing in his pursuit of greed, of selfishness, of all the things that lead him toward your enemy, has suddenly turned around and is listening."

My heart rejoices. The air is filled with incense, which the trees, wild and cultivated, are offering the Lord. Its fragrance is almost incredible.

As I look from the heights, I see people gathered together around a bishop or a priest, and I hear the chants of a choir jubilantly proclaiming the Creed. I seem suspended between heaven and earth, because I never expected this to happen, though I prayed that it would.

However, there are dark clouds gathering somewhere. On one hand I hear the Credo sung beautifully, and on the other hand I hear the moans and cries of the dying. While some people are singing the Credo, I turn my head and see killing. Dark clouds burst and seem to be raining dead people. I have never seen so many dead people, even when I was in a war. They come from everywhere. Newspapers declare deaths: a hundred a day here, two hundred there. Martyrs seem to be ascending the golden stairs that the blacks used to sing about.

I don't know what to do. My heart rejoices for those who sing the Credo and walk in the footsteps of Christ. My heart dies a thousand deaths, and is bathed in its own tears, because one brother is killing another brother. I am bewildered and lost. The beautiful incense offered to God by all the trees and bushes is somehow mixed with the scent of death.

I had already been preparing myself to follow in Christ's footsteps of pain. That is a Russian idea, of course, but probably also the idea of all Catholics: that the joy of Easter is followed by the pain of the Cross, and the pain of the Cross is followed by the joy of Easter. It is a circle that is unbreakable for anyone who believes in God. I believe in him. I believe in him with my whole heart, my whole mind, my whole being.

True, it is considered stupid to believe in God today. But I don't care! I proclaim to all and sundry that I am in love with God, and I call everybody to become in love with God. The wind carries my voice far and wide.

I cry out with a weak voice that shakes with pain, a voice that the wind picks up and amplifies loudly without any electrical instruments. I hear my very own voice far away, somewhere in China, somewhere in Africa, but above all, right here in this country.

I pray to the Lord of love to open the doors of human hearts. I know he cannot do it unless they let him, but I do what I can; I fall flat on the ground and implore him that they may open their hearts to his love.

The winds come, as they always do, and a voice, the same voice I always hear, says to me, "Think now of the resurrection. See, all the trees come back to life. People who have died will come back to life, too. Now is the time to sing your Alleluias."

Yes, today is the day of the Resurrection. A few days ago at his Last Supper, Christ said, "This is my body; this is my blood." He told us we must always re-enact this mystery in his name, in the reality of the immense faith that he gives to those who want it.

He also said that he was giving us a new commandment: that we should love one another as he loved us. How is that possible? How is it possible for a human being to love like he did? By what miracle does this possibility enter my heart and your heart? Since he said it, evidently it *is* possible.

The winds are getting stronger. Through them I hear a message of peace and joy. God says to me, "Yes, it is true. I have come to life. The tomb is empty, Catherine. There is no need to go there. Because now I am in everybody. So if you love anybody, you love me too. That is the message. To help you spread it, I give you, with all my love, the Bread and the Wine that will sustain you."

Afterword

There is a similarity between certain Old Testament prophets and holy fools. One aspect of both vocations is that of "reproaching the world." Catherine's message in *Uródivoi*, like that of many Old Testament prophets, is not easy to hear, nor easy to speak.

The prophet Jeremiah (Jer 20:7–9) speaks or rather complains about what this 'reproaching' costs:

> I am a laughing-stock all day long,
> they all make fun of me.
> For whenever I speak, I have to howl
> and proclaim, 'Violence and ruin!'
> For me, God's word has been the cause
> of insult and derision all day long.
>
> I would say to myself,
> 'I will not think about him,
> I will not speak in his name any more,'
> but then there seemed to be a fire
> burning in my heart,
> imprisoned in my bones.
> The effort to restrain it wearied me,
> I could not do it.

The commentary in the art calendar, *Icons and Holiness*, (St. Paul Media Productions UK, Middle Green, Slough, England, 1992) on the icon print of the Russian uródivoi, Basil the Blessed, reads:

> Holy fools live out the 'folly of the cross' literally, and are indifferent to human respect and judgements. They freely embrace an exterior form of folly and eccentricity, abandoning normal prudence and foresight.
>
> From early Christian times the charism of folly for Christ was recognized and placed side by side with the folly of the martyrs who renounced the supreme value of life to bear witness that Christ is the only value worth living for. A prime characteristic of 'fools for Christ' is their extreme freedom, which allows them to reproach and correct in a fraternal way even the rich and powerful, starting from that one foundation which is the love of Christ.

Basil the Blessed, a holy fool canonized by the Russian Orthodox Church, lived in Moscow without a roof over his head and spent many of his nights in prayer on the porches of churches. He was very beloved. In an early biography, it is related that, "whether in summer or winter, he wore neither clothes nor footwear, like primitive man in the earthly paradise before sin entered the world."

Afterword

Holy foolishness is a genuine calling from God. The fool can reach people where other forms of holiness, such as good teaching, cannot.

Holy fools are often playful and joking, but always for the spiritual benefit of others. The medieval fool or court jester could tell the king bitter truths about himself which would be unacceptable from others.

Fools in Christ frequently manifest the gift of prophecy, and some people are converted through fulfilled prophecies.

Holy fools are also distinguished by an interior freedom, partly won by an acquired imperviousness to physical suffering and hardships. Their asceticism includes abstinence from food and sleep, and indifference to the elements. Some holy fools in Russia walked half naked in all climatic conditions and had no roof over their heads, even where winters are severe.

They imitate the humiliation and kenosis or self-emptying of Christ; holy fools imitate the Divine Fool. (The gospel of Mark relates that Jesus' relatives "set out to take charge of him; they said, 'He is out of his mind.'" Mark 3:21) They also imitate Christ in his compassion for sinners.

Holy fools often associate with the poor and outcasts, and become one with them; they are an icon of Christ. They remain a stranger in the place where they live, and their personality remains unknown or hidden.

Fools for Christ are especially popular in Russian spirituality, but the Greek Orthodox Church has canonized holy fools, most notably St. Simeon of Emesa, who lived in the 6th century, and St. Andrew, in the 9th. Readers of Tolstoy may recall his description of "God's fool," Grisha.

Among the Roman Catholics whom Catherine considered as fools for Christ are St. Francis of Assisi and his Franciscan Brother, Juniper; St. Joseph Labre; Dorothy Day and Peter Maurin. Certain aspects of foolishness for God, like being indifferent to ridicule, are really the vocation of all of us, Catherine would say.

Holy foolishness is found in St. Paul's First Letter to the Corinthians.

> Christ sent me . . . to preach the gospel, and not by means of wisdom of language, wise words which would make the cross of Christ pointless. *The message of the cross is folly for those who are on the way to ruin, but for those of us who are on the road to salvation it is the power of God.* (1 Cor 1:17-18)

> As scripture says: 'I am going to destroy the wisdom of the wise and bring to nothing the understanding of any who understand.' Where are the philosophers? Where are the experts? . . . Do you not see how God has shown up human wisdom as folly? (1 Cor 1: 19-20)

> *Since in the wisdom of God the world was unable to recognise God through wisdom, it was God's pleasure to save believers through the folly of the gospel.* (1 Cor 1: 21)

> While the Jews demand miracles and the Greeks look for wisdom, we are preaching a crucified Christ: to the Jews an obstacle

they cannot get over, to the gentiles foolishness, but to those who have been called, whether they are Jews or Greeks, a Christ who is both the power of God and the wisdom of God. (1 Cor 1: 22-24)

God's folly is wiser than human wisdom, and God's weakness is stronger than human strength. (1 Cor 1: 25)

Any one who thinks he is wise by worldly standards must learn to be a fool in order to be really wise. (1 Cor 3: 18)

In response to promptings of the Holy Spirit, Catherine Doherty interiorized the calling of "foolishness for Christ," adapting it to modern life. However this was only one of the many facets of her vocation. Through her other books which reflect Russian or Eastern spirituality, readers may see how she also adapted the traditional callings to *Poustinia* and *Sobornost* and *Strannik* and *Molchanie* for today's secular world.

For further information about fools for Christ, we recommend the chapter, "The Fool in Christ as Prophet and Apostle," in Bishop Kallistos Ware's book, *The Inner Kingdom*, Vol. 1 of the Collected Works (2000, St. Vladimir's Seminary Press, 275 Scarsdale Road, Crestwood, N.Y. 10707-1699).

About the Author

Catherine de Hueck Doherty was born into a wealthy family in Russia in 1896. Many different strands of Christianity were woven into the spiritual fabric of her family background, but it was from the liturgy of the Russian Orthodox Church, the living faith of her father and mother, and the earthy piety of the Russian people themselves that Catherine received the powerful spiritual traditions and symbols of the Christian East.

At fifteen Catherine was married to Boris de Hueck. Soon they were swept into the devastating battles of World War I, where she served as a nurse. After the Revolution of 1917 they endured with all the peoples of the Russian Empire the agonies of starvation and civil war. Eventually Catherine and Boris escaped to England. At the beginning of her new life in the West, Catherine accepted the teachings of the Catholic Church, without rejecting the spiritual wealth of her Orthodox heritage.

In 1921 the couple sailed to Canada, where Catherine gave birth to their son George, soon after their arrival in Toronto. As refugees, they experienced dire poverty for a few years but soon Catherine's intelligence, energy, and gift for public speaking brought her to the attention of a large lecture bureau. Her talks were popular all across Canada and the United States. Within a few years, she became an executive with another, international lecture service. She became a North American success story.

In the 1930's, after several years of anguish, Catherine and Boris separated permanently; later the Church annulled their marriage. As devastated as Catherine was, she knew that God wanted something new from her now, but she did not know what it was. The words of Christ haunted her: "Sell all you possess, and give it to the poor, and come, follow Me."

Catherine took a room in a slum section of Toronto and began to quietly love and serve her neighbors, becoming their friend, and praying, hidden in their midst. But when others saw her and heard her speak, they wanted to join her. There was an intensity to her faith and love that lit a flame in the hearts of many men and women. Catherine had not envisaged a community, but when the Archbishop told her that, yes, Christ was calling her to this, she accepted, and soon Friendship House was born.

The works of Friendship House were modest—a shelter for the homeless, meals for the hungry, recreation and books for the young, a newspaper to make known the social teachings of the Church. Catherine initiated an interracial apostolate in Harlem, living with and serving the African-Americans. This work expanded to other cities: Chicago, Washington, D.C., and Portland, Oregon. Friendship House became well known in the American Church.

Catherine shared with her friend, Dorothy Day of the Catholic Worker, the intense struggle to move the Gospel out of books into believers' lives. Even if a few friends, such as the young Thomas Merton, recognized in her the power of the Holy Spirit and an unwavering fidelity to Christ's Church, many others were frightened by her Russian bluntness. Others simply could not grasp the largeness of her vision, especially because her experience of the ways of God were so foreign to them. Finally after a painful difference of opinion over the nature of the Friendship House Apostolate, Catherine found herself pushed again into the chartless waters of the Lord.

This time Catherine did not have to start alone. In 1943 she had married Eddie Doherty, a celebrated newspaperman, after he convinced her and her bishop that he wanted to share and support her vocation. In 1947, then, Catherine and Eddie came to Combermere, a small village northeast of Toronto, where the Bishop of Pembroke had agreed she could work among the rural families.

Again others came to join Catherine, and this time priests came to stay as well. The apostolate, now called Madonna House, grew slowly, but by the year 2000 Madonna House has more than 210 members, including twenty priests. The apostolate has foundations in Russia, England, France, Belgium, Brazil, Grenada, Ghana and Liberia, in addition to fourteen others in Canada and the United States. The training center in Combermere, Ontario offers an experience of Gospel life to hundreds every year.

As Catherine's inner life deepened and the community matured, she shared the fullness of the inner vocation Christ had formed in her. On the eve of the Second Vatican Council in 1962, Catherine established the West's first poustinia—a desert place of fasting and praying for unity, in, with and through Christ, a unity "that could only be the fruit of love." Her book *Poustinia* was awarded the prestigious *Prix Goncourt* of the *Academie Français*, and has been translated into dozens of languages; it witnesses to her spiritual depth and passionate zeal to pass on her faith in God.

Catherine died in 1985, a woman who had become a spiritual giant by responding to grace.

If you would like to learn more about Catherine Doherty and Madonna House, please visit our Internet web site at: www.madonnahouse.org

About the Cover Painting

In the other books in the *Madonna House Classics* series, the cover scene was set on the island in which Catherine lived in a little cabin or "poustinia" for many years. Now, in *Uródivoi*, the scene changes dramatically. The island has receded, as its inner mission has been accomplished.

The heart first entered the desert (*Poustinia*) to meet God in Scripture and solitude. Having allowed God to cleanse it thoroughly, it became one with the Trinity (*Sobornost*). God then beckons the soul, transformed by love, to become a pilgrim (*Strannik*), going forth into the silence of God (*Molchanie*). Now, in *Uródivoi*, the final journey is being made. The soul is called to move from the sea of silence into the hearts of our brothers and sisters in the 'marketplace'—the world.

In *Uródivoi*, we are invited to open the doors of our hearts to the Lord of Love, to the foolishness of the Cross, becoming a fool for the sake of Christ, even as he became a fool for our sake. "For God's foolishness is wiser than human wisdom." (1 Cor. 1:25)

The painting was created in 1993 by Patrick Stewart, a member of the Madonna House Apostolate.

Also by Catherine Doherty

Madonna House Classics Series:

Poustinia: Encountering God in Silence, Solitude and Prayer
Sobornost: Experiencing Unity of Mind, Heart and Soul
Strannik: The Call to the Pilgrimage of the Heart
Molchanie: The Silence of God
Uródivoi: Holy Fools
Bogoroditza: She Who Gave Birth to God

Other Titles:

Dear Father: A Message of Love to Priests
Dear Parents
Dear Seminarian
Dearly Beloved: Letters to the Children of My Spirit
Donkey Bells: Advent and Christmas
Doubts, Loneliness, Rejection
Fragments of My Life: A Memoir
The Gospel of a Poor Woman
The Gospel Without Compromise
Grace in Every Season
Kiss of Christ
My Russian Yesterdays
Not Without Parables
Season of Mercy: Lent and Easter
Soul of My Soul
Welcome, Pilgrim

MADONNA HOUSE PUBLICATIONS
Combermere • Ontario • Canada • K0J 1L0

The aim of our publications is to share the Gospel of Jesus Christ with all people from all walks of life.

It is to awaken and deepen in our readers an experience of God's love in the most simple and ordinary facets of everyday life.

It is to make known to our readers how to live the tender, saving life of God in everything they do and for everyone they meet.

Our publications are dedicated to Our Lady of Combermere, the Mother of Jesus and of His Church, and we are under her protection and care.

Madonna House Publications is a non-profit apostolate of Madonna House within the Catholic Church. Donations allow us to send books to people who cannot afford them but most need them all around the world. Thank you for your participation in this apostolate.

To request a catalogue of our current publications, please call (613) 756-3728, or write to us at:

> Madonna House Publications
> 2888 Dafoe Rd
> Combermere ON   K0J 1L0
> Canada

You can also visit us on the Internet at the following address:

> www.madonnahouse.org